Introduction by Major Iv...

After the Civil War ended in 1649, Pembroke... Local people used the stone for building the... only in the late nineteenth century that the celebrated antiquarian, ... Cobb, acquired the castle and devoted three years to the care and partial restoration of this noble fortress. Thereafter the castle was once again neglected until in 1928 my grandfather, Major-General Sir Ivor Philipps, purchased it and for the remaining twelve years of his life undertook an extensive and ambitious restoration programme. The private trust that my mother, Mrs. Basil Ramsden, formed thirty years ago continues this work. The Trust has also embarked on a programme of interpretation of the history of the castle and the lives of those who lived here. This outstanding interpretative exhibition has been organised by Mr. Neil Ludlow and, I am sure, it will be of great interest to our visitors.

An introductory video and an exhibition of the history of the Pembroke Yeomanry has also been recently established in the gatehouse.

The Trust takes pride in presenting a monument in as good a state of preservation as any in Wales. Trustees and staff welcome you to Pembroke Castle and hope that you will enjoy your visit. Please take every care to avoid accidents and parents/guardians are requested to be with small children at all times.

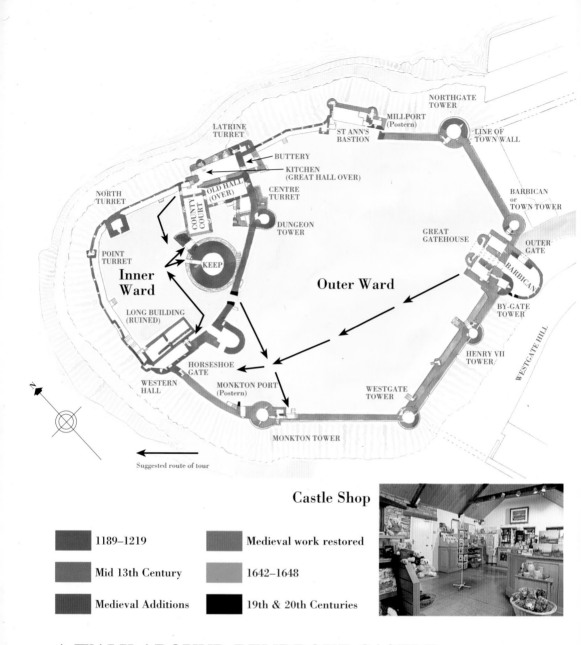

NORTHGATE TOWER

MILLPORT (Postern)

LATRINE TURRET

ST ANN'S BASTION

LINE OF TOWN WALL

BUTTERY

KITCHEN (GREAT HALL OVER)

NORTH TURRET

OLD HALL (OVER)

CENTRE TURRET

BARBICAN or TOWN TOWER

COUNTY COURT

DUNGEON TOWER

GREAT GATEHOUSE

OUTER GATE

POINT TURRET

KEEP

BARBICAN

Inner Ward

Outer Ward

BY-GATE TOWER

LONG BUILDING (RUINED)

HENRY VII TOWER

WESTGATE HILL

HORSESHOE GATE

WESTERN HALL

MONKTON PORT (Postern)

WESTGATE TOWER

N

MONKTON TOWER

Suggested route of tour

Castle Shop

1189–1219	Medieval work restored
Mid 13th Century	1642–1648
Medieval Additions	19th & 20th Centuries

A WALK AROUND PEMBROKE CASTLE

Approach the Castle from the town centre or walk up Westgate Hill from the car park below the ramparts. Tickets are obtainable from the Castle Shop. Enter the Castle by passing the cenotaph through the arch and turn right through the massive Gatehouse and Barbican which formerly had three portcullises and great wooden doors reinforced with iron draw-bars. This building will be explored later for it is best to make a tour logically, starting from the Inner Gatehouse then on to the Keep.

INNER GATEHOUSE AND KEEP

Facing you across the flat surface of lawn and tarmac of the Outer Ward is the massive form of the round Keep. Like the Round Tower at Windsor this is the dominant feature of Pembroke Castle. It was built soon after 1200 by William Marshal Earl of Pembroke. It was well-nigh impregnable and, had the other towers and outer walls been taken, the garrison would have made this Keep their last refuge. The walls are 19 feet thick at the base and the Keep rises to 75 feet in height and is crowned with a stone dome set as a centre-piece in a triple crown of parapet and turret.

Enter the lower door and look up. It is an awe-inspiring sight. It is possible in good weather to climb to the top where marvellous views over Pembrokeshire can be had. This climb should be avoided in high winds.

The original main entrance was on the first floor and the wide steps up are a reconstruction of the 14th or 15th century addition.

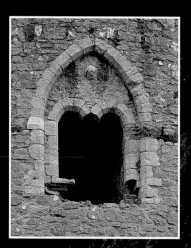

One of the windows
of the Keep

Part of the magnificent
re-construction in the
Gatehouse Museum which
evokes how the castle looked
in its heyday

The Keep, 75ft high and 50ft in diameter, is the largest – and finest – of its kind in the country. It had 5 floors beneath a stone dome that is unique in Britain – as are the 2 tiers of parapet and central turret. It was originally entered through a first floor doorway reached by a timber stair.

Line drawing by Neil Ludlow

THE CHANCERY OR COUNTY COURT

Turn right out of the Keep entrance and on your right the remains of a late 13th or early 14th century gabled building will be seen. Outlines of the high-pitched roof can be traced. This section of the building was recorded in 1331. It was the part of the Castle where business would be conducted, accounts kept and where the county court of the Palatinate was held.

Go through the arch at the end to see the Northern Hall.

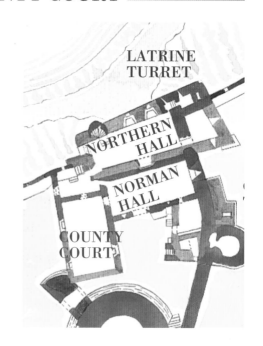

THE NORTHERN HALL

This impressive chamber and its huge decorated windows date from about 1280-1290. It is easy to see the holes in the stonework for the wooden joists where a floor would have been and the two huge fireplaces, one above the other, share the chimney. These were obviously living rooms for members of the family. There is another exit from the Northern Hall, perhaps unique in British castles. As you enter, on the left, there is a doorway leading to a long downward-leading spiral staircase. At the base of this is a surprise. It is the most extraordinary feature of Pembroke Castle.

THE NORTHERN HALL

At the bottom of this staircase is an immense natural cave formed aeons ago by swirling waters in the limestone rock. It looks out over the river and through this cave access to the Castle by water would have been possible and the cavern itself was once used as a boat store. The lateral dimensions are 80 feet by 60 feet with a lofty roof.

THE NORMAN HALL

Ascend the spiral staircase back into the Northern
Hall and back through the arch to enter the
Norman Hall which lies adjacent. This is
sometimes known as the Old Hall and was built
at the same time as the Keep itself or
possibly even earlier by Richard
Strongbow. Notice the remains of the
large fireplace on the
south wall. There is a
large double latrine
chamber to the
south east -
a later
addition.

Next to the Norman Hall is the
small private room with its Oriel
window added by Jasper Tudor.

THE DUNGEON TOWER

Turn left through the wide arch of the Norman Hall. The Keep faces you and to the left is the Dungeon Tower added to the inner curtain wall by de Valence. Climb the stairs and into the tower. In a corner of the chamber is a sinister illuminated hole in the ground. This was an oubliette - a hole where prisoners were cast and literally forgotten. There was no access other than from the hole.

A latrine turret was also added at this time. A staircase leads to the domed roof with views over the river and the Gatehouse. Return to the ground floor.

THE WESTERN HALL, CHAPEL AND INNER GATEHOUSE

Keep the wall of the Keep on your left and as you emerge, the Western Hall and Tower will be seen across the grass over towards the left. As you approach the building notice the remains of the Inner Curtain Wall on the left. To the right of the Western Hall are the excavated ruins of the Chapel. A worn step and door socket can still be seen at the entrance. The Inner Gatehouse once formed a fortified

gatehouse guarding the Inner Ward before the Outer Ward was built. Inside the Western Hall there is a long vaulted chamber with a large fireplace on the south wall. Notice the arrow slits and the latrine or garderobe in a turret to the north west. Here again there is a staircase to the roof. Notice, at the top, the stone chimneystack.

View from Westgate Tower of Monkton Tower (centre) and of Western Hall and the excavated ruins of the Chapel to the right

Monkton Tower with Monkton Priory seen in the background

MONKTON TOWER

As you come out of the Western Hall you pass from the Inner Ward to the Outer Ward and as you make your way towards the outer curtain wall and Monkton Tower you walk over the foundation, which is all that remains, of the Inner Gate House. At one point the ground falls away and a small portion of the limestone bedrock on which the castle was built can be seen. Before the Outer Ward was built the original castle buildings - the Keep, the Dungeon Tower, Norman Hall, Inner Gatehouse, etc. would be approached via the main street of the town which at the time would have come right up to the Inner Gate. When the Outer Ward was built the pathway was obliterated and the new outer curtain wall was built over it. A new entrance was created and this was called the Water Port. Hard by is Monkton Tower. From now on you can approach the towers either from the ground or by way of an upper walkway. There is much to be seen in the rooms and passages between here and the Gatehouse.

The first of these towers is Monkton Tower, so called because it commands a view of Monkton Priory on the other side of the water best seen from the very top. Notice the restored fireplace.

MONKTON TOWER

WESTGATE TOWER

To see the rest of the Tower you have to approach it from the other side. A short flight of steps leads into a small room which may at one time have housed prisoners. Some graffiti can be seen etched into the stonework. Some of the doodling looks heraldic. If you do not want to descend to ground level, follow the curtain wall towards the Westgate Tower.

WESTGATE TOWER

Pembroke was once a walled town and this tower overlooked one of the town's fortified towers - the old West Gate. The tower was severely damaged in the Civil War but was restored in 1931. The West Gate itself has long since vanished but some of the remains of the walls can be traced at the edge of the garden opposite. The wall between the Gatehouse and the Westgate Tower was strengthened in the 17th century.

NEIL LUDLOW'S STUNNING RECREATION OF HOW THE CASTLE LOOKED IN LATE 14th CENTURY

KEEP

COUNTY COURT

NORTHERN HALL

HENRY VII TOWER

HENRY VII TOWER

The next tower is known as the Henry VII tower as it is believed to be the birthplace of Henry Tudor, Earl of Richmond, afterwards King Henry VII. It is known for certain that Henry was born at Pembroke and the most likely candidate for the bedroom where he first saw the light is the room in this tower containing the magnificent fireplace. This is much restored but did have traces of some heraldic ornamentation. The antiquarian John Leland, an older contemporary of King Henry, visited the Castle and noted that the chimneypiece was ornamented with the arms and badges of the first Tudor King. He wrote: 'In the outer Ward I saw the chamber where King Henry VII was born, in knowledge whereof a chimney is new made with the arms and badges of King Henry VII'.

It is not entirely certain that this is the actual room where Henry Tudor was born, but it seems to be the most likely. Leland was writing in about 1538 and could have talked to old men whose fathers or grandfathers were around at the time of Henry's birth in 1457. When the fireplace was installed and bedecked with Tudor heraldry there must have been a very strong tradition that this was the birthplace, although other traditions existed.

Henry VII
by Michiel Sitlow
by courtesy of the
National Portrait
Gallery, London

There are three floors: the lower ground floor (semi-basement) with steps up to the first floor; the first floor with steps to the second floor which also has entrances from the ramparts.

From the top of the Tower there are good views of the main street of Pembroke and the church tower.

The Henry VII Tower was severely damaged during the Civil War and most of it has been extensively restored.

THE GATEHOUSE & BY-GATE TOWER

You are now about to enter the most impressive of the later buildings of Pembroke Castle - the Gatehouse. This, with its adjacent Barbican Tower, form a fortified unit larger than many complete castles. The Gatehouse was an important residential part of the Castle. The rooms are large and were roofed with timber and lead. The bare stone walls would, perhaps, have been hung with arrases depicting hunting scenes and there would be rushes on the floors.

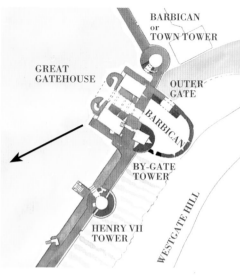

The Barbican Entrance

Furniture would have been basic - a few chairs and a table. If there had been no glass available for the windows, heavy wooden shutters would have helped keep out the cold with flickering rush-lights on the walls. Large tree-trunks would be blazing in the fireplaces and in winter it could be cosy, though it is difficult to imagine this now.

The western half of the Gatehouse extends to form the By-Gate Tower, rebuilt in 1934, and this leads into a long chamber where exhibitions are mounted. The ground floor includes a guard room and a strongly-built stone arched dungeon, access to which is obtained through the Guard Room.

THE BARBICAN TOWER

Immediately east of the Gatehouse is the Barbican Tower with walls nine feet thick. This tower suffered very badly in the Civil War. After its final capture by Cromwell 'Old Noll' tried to blow it up. Its great strength against a weapon which was unknown when the Castle was built says much for the medieval architects and builders and it survived enough, though much mutilated, to allow a restoration in the 1930s. From the top fine views are to be had and there are several rooms to see.

Barbican and Gatehouse are joined by a first floor passage. You can now descend to ground level and examine the exterior of these massive towers.

THE GATEHOUSE MUSEUM

Interpretative exhibition of the Seat of the Earls of Pembroke, designed by Neil Ludlow

A model of the Gatehouse of the original timber castle, 1100

Model of Inner Ward in stone and Outer Ward still in timber (Models made by Eric Bradforth – Tenby)

Trustees thought it appropriate to establish a museum and exhibition of the last invasion of mainland Britain – Fishguard 1797 and of the Pembroke Yeomanry as the regiment was commanded by Colonel Ivor Philipps DSO, MP from 1908–1914. The Colonel went on to command the 38th Welsh Division in the Great War and acquired by purchase the castle in 1928.

Right: Reconstruction of The 30th Company Imperial Yeomanry (Pembroke Yeomanry) in action at Kaffir Kop, South Africa 1901

NORTH GATE TOWER

Continue the tour by keeping the castle wall on your right and you will see ahead North Gate Tower. It once overlooked the old North Gate of the town walls but this was demolished in 1820. The tower has two floors with some good rooms and fireplaces. Access to the walls is from the second floor.

MILL PORT

The walls now turn north west so that the Keep, Dungeon Tower and adjacent buildings come head on into view to form an impressive sight. A gap in the wall, known as Mill Port, gave access to a flour-mill powered by the once tidal inlet below. Mill Port was protected by North Gate Tower and St. Anne's bastion so that food might be brought into the Castle in difficult moments, particularly during a long siege.

ST. ANNE'S BASTION

The last architectural feature of note to be seen is St. Anne's Bastion – a long narrow hall with a turret at each end. Cromwell pounded the walls here with his artillery which was positioned opposite on the other side of the river. The damage would have been hurriedly and inexpertly repaired at the time and in this century the place was in crumbling ruins until restored in 1929. The long narrow hall itself was also repaired and four years later had been made into a small, comfortable dwelling. It has now been put to yet another use, in housing the Castle's main lavatories.

This ends the tour of Pembroke Castle. It is not possible to take it all in on a single visit, so we hope you will visit again and become more familiar with one of Wales's most spectacular buildings.

THE HISTORY OF PEMBROKE CASTLE

Pembroke has one of the largest castles in Wales. Despite its size and impressive appearance, it was not a royal castle but the possession of a private lord. And while like most private castles in Britain it was primarily a residence and administrative centre of the lords territories, Pembroke Castle's fortifications were continually extended throughout its history and it displays stonework from many periods.

Soon after defeating the English at the Battle of Hastings in 1066, the Norman invaders turned to Wales. Their conquest of Wales, however, was piecemeal; it was not until 1093 that Earl Roger de Montgomery swept into West Wales from Shrewsbury and built the first castle at Pembroke. Like many of his period, Roger's castle was built of timber; under his son Arnulf it was the base of subjugation of the surrounding country, despite being twice besieged by the Welsh.

In 1102 the Norman King Henry I took possession of Pembroke Castle and the lordship established by Arnulf became state property. He increased Norman control, deliberately founding a town at the castle gate with a market, quay and mint.

William Marshal, Earl of Pembroke from his tomb in Temple Church

The surrounding country was in fact colonised with Flemish emigrés, Religious domination, that had begun under Arnulf who established a Priory just over the river at Monkton, increased with the construction of a church within the town. In 1138 King Stephen created the earldom of Pembroke for Gilbert de Clare, known as 'Strongbow'. The Castle was still a fairly basic structure then of wooden palisades. Gilbert was succeeded by his son Richard de Clare 2nd Earl of Pembroke, also known as 'Strongbow'. Richard was instrumental in the Norman conquest of Ireland. He married Eva, daughter of the King of Leinster, and on the King's death was crowned as his successor. He left an only daughter and heiress Isabel who remained a ward of Henry II until the King married her off to William Marshal who, in right of his wife, became Earl of Pembroke in 1189. Pembrokeshire remained a self-governing region (palatinate) right up until the reign of Henry VIII and the King's writ was unknown in the area except when issued by the Crown whenever the earldom fell vacant. The Earls had their own courts (in Pembroke Castle's Chancery) and dispensed their own justice.

William Marshal Earl of Pembroke, was a mighty figure in medieval England and Wales. A crusader and faithful adherent of Henry II, he championed the causes of

both Richard I and John, advising the latter upon Magna Carta. He was also Regent to Henry III during that King's infancy. William Marshal's chief legacy to Pembroke was the construction in stone of the Great Tower (Keep) and much of the Inner Ward. He was succeeded in turn by each of his five sons.

William Marshal II, the eldest son of the first Marshal Earl, was a trusted supporter of John's successor, Henry III, and brought over a force of Irish to suppress a Welsh uprising led by Prince Llewellyn ap Iorwerth. Eventually the King presided over an agreement between Earl and Prince whereby the latter was handed Cardigan and Carmarthen. At his death William was succeeded by his brother, Richard Earl of Pembroke who was not in favour at the English Court. Henry III refused to allow Richard to succeed to the estates which led to the latter having to lay siege to his own castle to gain possession. Richard was murdered in Ireland in 1234 and was succeeded by his brother Gilbert, Earl of Pembroke. It was he who greatly enlarged and strengthened the Castle. Gilbert fell from his horse in 1241 whilst jousting during a tournament and was killed. He was succeeded by his brother Walter, the penultimate Earl of Pembroke of the Marshal family. Walter took a great interest in his Castle and no doubt

Melusine, the serpent-fairy ancestress of the Lusignans

would have carried out many improvements and modernisations had he lived to enjoy his patrimony long enough. As it was he died four years later to be succeeded by his last surviving brother Anselm who survived for but 18 (some say only 11) days. His death, childless, fulfilled a curse put upon the first William Marshal by an Irish bishop whom Marshal had wronged. He cursed the Earl and said that all his sons would die childless.

William Marshal did, however, have several daughters who escaped the curse and the great Marshal properties were distributed amongst them. Pembroke Castle went to Joan who herself had a daughter, another Joan, who married William de Valence. William was half-brother of Henry III, being a son of Isabella d'Angoulême (widow of King John) by her second husband Hugh de Lusignan. Through his marriage Valence became Lord of Pembroke but was never formally created Earl.

William de Valence's family, the Lusignans, provided Kings of Cyprus and Jerusalem. They claimed descent from an ancestral spirit, Melusine, who was normal on every day of the week except Saturdays when she became half woman and half serpent. When her Lusignans husband discovered her secret she flew from a window in Lusignans Castle and was never seen again!

In those days, when danger threatened, the townsfolk would huddle within the castle walls for protection and indeed William built the walls and towers around the Outer Ward. During the more peaceful days of Edward I they asked their lord and master to fortify the town of Pembroke to avoid having to rely on the Castle, and this William de Valence did. There were three main gates and a postern - only fragments of these walls remain but their gates are reflected in the names of two of the castle's towers; the Westgate Tower and the Northgate Tower.

Earl William died in 1296 in France but was brought home for burial at Westminster. He was succeeded by his son Aymer, Earl of Pembroke who, like his father, was a warring soldier but also a diplomat. He defeated the Scots at Ruthven in 1306 but shared in the defeat at Bannockburn eight years later. He died without issue in Paris while on an embassy mission to Charles IV. During the de Valence tenure of Pembroke Castle, lasting some 70 years, much building work was carried out. When Aymer died so did the male line of that branch of the family. His sister had married John de Hastings and their son, Laurence, became Earl

The tomb of William de Valence Earl of Pembroke in Westminster Abbey

of Pembroke but died before taking possession. Laurence's son John, who served with the Black Prince in France, succeeded as second Earl of the Hastings line. He died soldiering in France in 1375 and was, in turn, succeeded by his son, also John. This John was but a callow youth and died in 1389 at the age of 17, thus ending an inheritance by blood of about 280 years since the earldom was created for Gilbert de Clare back in the reign of King Stephen. The earldom now lapsed to the Crown in the person of Richard II, and thenceforward constables were appointed by the Crown.

In 1400, the great Welsh hero, soldier and patriot, Owain Glyndwr, led yet another insurrection against the hated English settlers. Pembroke escaped a siege through the Constable at the time, Francis à Court, buying off Glyndwr with the Welsh equivalent of danegeld.

By then Richard II had been recently deposed by the usurper Henry Bolingbroke, who became King Henry IV. The new King's fourth son, Humphrey Bolingbroke, was created Duke of Gloucester by his father. When Henry V succeeded, he made his brother, Gloucester, Earl of Pembroke.

He served with the young Harry at Harfleur and was severely wounded at Agincourt: 'Then shall our names, familiar in his mouth as household words, Harry the King, Bedford and Exeter, Warwick and Talbot, Salisbury and Gloucester, be in their flowing cups freshly remembered'. This was the 'Gloucester' of those words put in the mouth of the King by Shakespeare in Henry V. Gloucester, however, was not popular with Margaret of Anjou (Henry VI's Queen) and she had him put in prison where he died in 1447.

Jasper Tudor became Earl of Pembroke in 1454. He was half-brother of Henry VI and second son of Owain Tewdwr and Queen Catherine of France. Jasper was the first to make Pembroke Castle more of a home than a fortress. He embellished the domestic buildings with fireplaces and a fine oriel window. Jasper's older brother, Edmund Earl of Richmond, married Lady Margaret Beaufort, daughter of John Beaufort, Duke of Somerset, a great-grandson of Edward III. During the Wars of the Roses Edmund sent his teenage pregnant wife to Pembroke for protection under the roof of his brother Jasper, Earl of Pembroke. On a visit to the Castle in 1456 he died and two months later the 15-year-old Margaret was laid up in a room in a tower and gave birth to a son, Henry Tewdwr, or as it has become, Tudor. This was in a room which is now known as the Henry VII Tower, for the child eventually, as Earl of Richmond, ended the Wars of the Roses by defeating Richard III at Bosworth Field and became, by right of battle if not by descent, King Henry VII of England,

first sovereign of the Tudor dynasty. The young man was brought up at Pembroke until he was fourteen when he was taken abroad with his mother by his uncle Jasper to live in Brittany during a siege by Sir Rhys ap Thomas. Jasper returned with his nephew in 1485 and after the victory against Richard III he was restored to his title and castle of Pembroke which had been temporarily removed from him and given to William Herbert and then to Prince Edward, son of Edward IV and one of the Princes in the Tower.

Henry VII never returned to Wales but he created his son Henry Prince of Wales Earl of Pembroke. That Henry, in turn, as Henry VIII, created Anne Boleyn Marchioness of Pembroke. It was, however, Henry himself who abolished the status of earldom and created the County of Pembroke.

Henry VII's mother, Margaret Beaufort, Countess of Richmond

For a time Pembroke Castle slumbered – a peaceful place, still an impressive fortress but without a role. It remained Crown property until the reign of James I. That king made a gift of the Castle to a favourite and it remained in private hands.

It was during the next reign that Pembroke Castle once again became a key factor, this time in the saddest conflict in which England and Wales were ever engaged – the Civil War. Although most of South Wales was Royalist, Pembroke was fortified and declared for Parliament. There were three key figures involved; the Mayor of Pembroke, John Poyer, Colonel Powell and Major General Laugharne. The Mayor, a man of means, paid for the defensive measures and the two officers prepared to do battle with the Royalists.

The Cavalier Lord Carbery, having captured Tenby, laid siege to Pembroke but was foiled by Parliamentary reinforcements arriving by sea at Milford Haven. The Roundheads then went on the offensive and took, among other castles, Haverfordwest, Tenby and Carew.

In 1648 there was a strange turnabout in fortunes. The Civil War was all but over and Cromwell ordered Laugharne to disband his forces in Pembroke. For some reason he refused. Poyer was unwilling to relinquish his post as Military Governor of the Castle. Lord Fairfax sent officers over to sort things out and occupied the town but they were evicted. Poyer, Powell and Laugharne declared for the King and won over many old Parliamentarians.